WHERE'S SANTA

Louis Shea

SCHOLASTIC

Everyone will have to journey through thousands of years to get back to now. Can you find each of these in every scene?

Santa

Santa should be getting ready for Christmas Eve—he's got a list to check and presents to pack! But now that Naughty Nat has been transported back in time, he needs to follow and find her instead. Can you spot Santa wherever *and whenever* he goes?

Naughty Nat

Nat's been on the naughty side of Santa's list for a while . . . but now she's really done it! Sneaking into Santa's workshop, taking his snow globe and then getting lost in time is probably not going to get her on Santa's nice side anytime soon. See if you can help Santa find where she is.

Elvy

Elvy has been known to cause the odd spot of mischief and mayhem himself. So when Santa asked for Elvy's help to find Naughty Nat, he jumped in the sleigh to trace the trail of trouble straightaway!

Mr Paws

Mr Paws might look like a sweet and innocent kitty, but he is always eager to join Nat in whatever naughty adventure she is plotting next. He wasn't quite expecting to go on a time-travelling trip though!

Fluffy

Santa's pet yeti, Fluffy, loves sneaking into the back of the sleigh to go flying with Santa—why should the reindeer have all the fun?! Now he's looking forward to meeting his ice-age ancestors on this wild ride!

Baby reindeer

Santa has lots of reindeer at the North Pole. It's hard to keep track of them all! So when this curious young'un followed Mr Paws into Santa's workshop, he was transported back in time too! Make sure you find him wherever they go.

Snow globe

Did you ever wonder how Santa manages to travel all over the world in just one night? Well, with the help of this special Go-Slow Snow Globe, Santa can adjust time! Find it in every scene—it's the only way to get everyone back.

Time-travelling scientist

It's not only Nat who has uncovered the mysteries of time travel. This kooky scientist has been tinkering with his time machine for a while now, and it looks like he's finally got it up and running. Can you spot where he pops up?

Sleigh

This trusty sleigh is the only way Santa likes to travel. So when Nat disappeared through the time vortex he immediately jumped into the sleigh to follow her. Make sure you find it—Santa will need it on Christmas Eve when he gets back!

Christmas tree

Santa will be happy to know that no matter where he goes in history, a Christmas tree will be there to remind him of his favourite time of year. They're even in space! See if you can help Santa find them all.

Dragonfly

Dragonflies have been around for ages and ages—literally! These little critters have been zipping about for millions of years, so you will be able to find one in every scene.

Diamond

Diamonds are forever! Actually, they're quite rare and hard to find, so Santa will have to look carefully for this sparkly gem wherever he goes—it will be the perfect present for Mrs Claus!

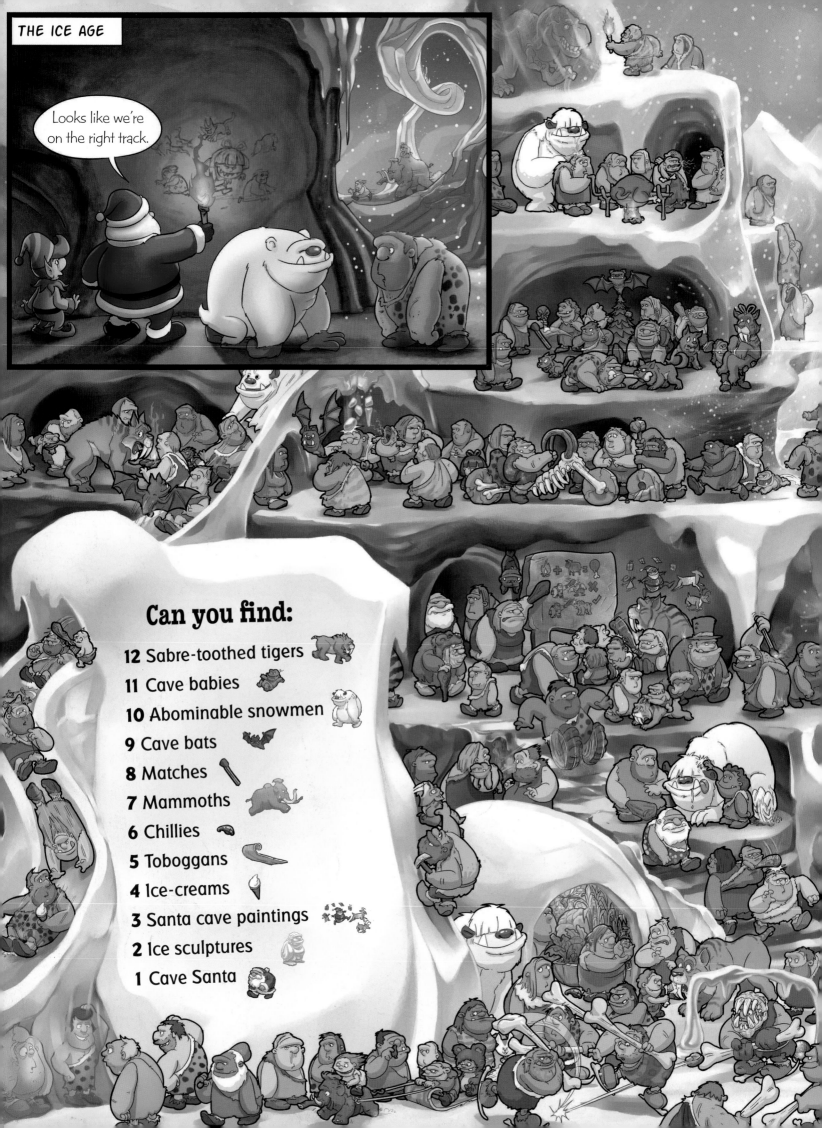

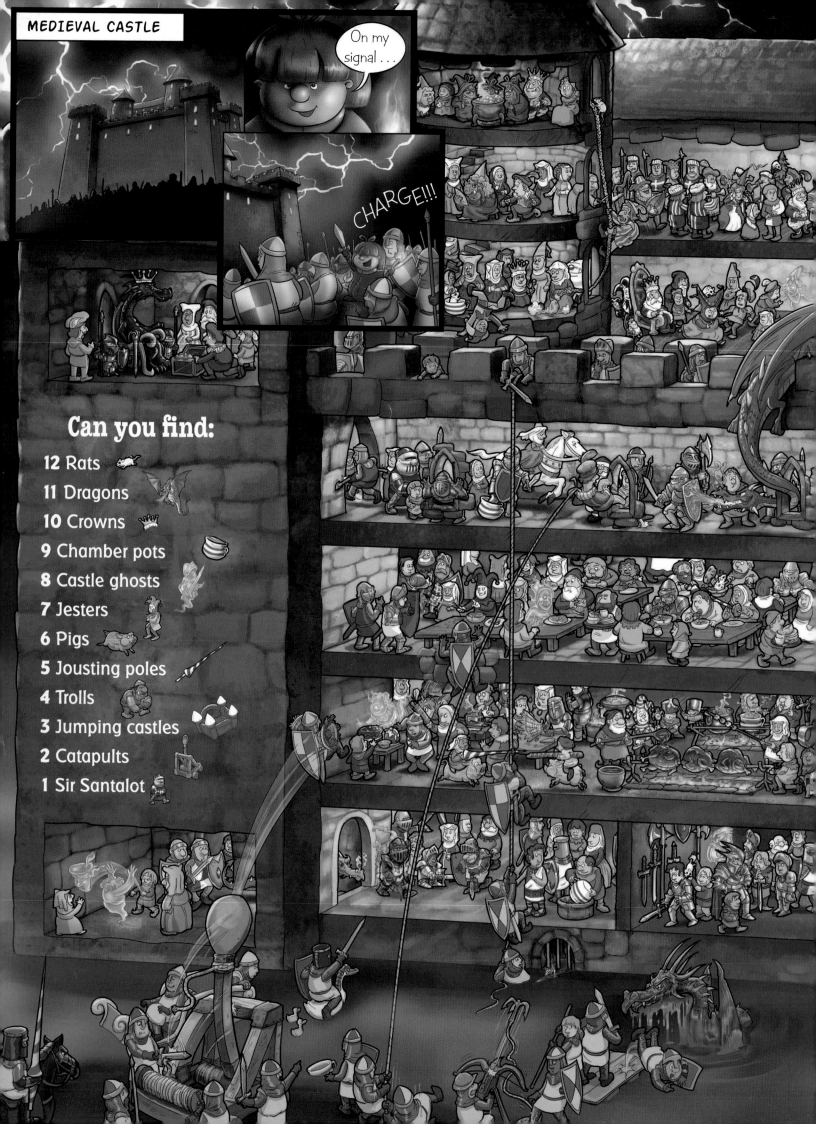

FINALLY, AFTER A VERY LONG DAY, SANTA RETURNS NAUGHTY NAT TO HER OWN HOME, IN HER OWN TIME.

For Kiyoko and Jethro — LS

Scholastic Children's Books,
Euston House, 24 Eversholt Street,
London NW1 1DB, UK

A division of Scholastic Ltd
London ~ New York ~ Toronto ~ Sydney ~ Auckland
Mexico City ~ New Delhi ~ Hong Kong

First published in Australia by Scholastic Australia, 2016
Published in the UK by Scholastic Ltd, 2017

Text and illustrations © Louis Shea, 2016

ISBN 978 1407 17861 5

Printed and bound in Malaysia

Papers used by Scholastic Children's Books are made from wood grown in sustainable forests.

scholastic.co.uk

Did you find the pink dinosaur in every scene?